EVERY
POSSIBLE
THING

Other works by Karen Poppy

Crack Open/Emergency, poetry chapbook
Finishing Line Press, 2020

our own beautiful brutality, poetry chapbook
Finishing Line Press, forthcoming

EVERY POSSIBLE THING

poems

KAREN POPPY

Homestead Lighthouse Press
Grants Pass, Oregon

ISBN 978-1-950475-07-0

Homestead Lighthouse Press
1668 NE Foothill Boulevard
Unit A
Grants Pass, OR 97526
www.homesteadlighthousepress.com

Distributed by Homestead Lighthouse Press, Amazon.com, Barnes & Noble, Daedalus Distribution.

Homestead Lighthouse Press gratefully acknowledges the generous support of its readers and patrons.

Book design by Ray Rhamey.

Cover photo by Neil Stalnaker, may he rest in peace and heavenly music, with thanks to him for inspiring through his music and art.

Author photo by Lorelei Ghanizadeh.

ACKNOWLEDGMENTS

I am grateful to the editors of the following journals, in which the poems in this book, sometimes in earlier versions, first appeared or are soon forthcoming:

ArLiJo: "New Moon"

Better than Starbucks: "I Like When You Speak"

Catamaran Literary Reader: "A Single Note in the Infinite"

The Cortland Review: "What We Find" and "Standing in the Kitchen"

Ecozon@: European Journal of Literature, Culture and Environment: "Pollination"

Peacock Journal: "Your Words"

Plainsongs "New Roots"

Queen's Mob Teahouse: "Badass Mermaid"

Wallace Stevens Journal: "Which to Prefer"

CONTENTS

Every Possible Thing

What I promised, I gave you:
Silver-skinned gloves, my hands
Loosened from life became twin fish.
Gold-skinned shoes, my tongue
Loosened from speech became bird song.

Dearest silk, you called my skin that,
Now may it suit you after my death.
All is possible, my love, my life
Given to you to take away any doubt,
Any moment lonely. I embrace you
Intimately. Wear me like finery.

Emily and Susie

The life a love can have
Before it dies, a rich
And lucky thing. Cashmere
Combed and honey-kissed—
An orchard of happiness.

That I'll wake there before
I die, to spend a day
Among that fruit—with you!
Then I'll not see eternity
As such a barren misery.

Virginia

I've survived everything,
Even my self-drowning.
I've emerged, singing,
Wiping mud from brow,
Learning how to breathe
Within this expansion,
Having broken free,
Free from every prison—
Even that of my own lungs.
In death, I am alive.
Stones don't weigh me down.
This river, a sea, an ocean
Awash in spirited sound,
Color, blue and green.
Water, swirl of ether, I
Exist here, polished clean.

Not Stamped Ephemeral

Come now,
Undulating snow
Unfurls before us.

We know
Our horses' hooves
Will move us through
As snow sings
Its angels.

What brings
Light
That hastens
Broken snow?

What brings
Yield
That returns
Fields now fallow?

As you say,
In nature,
Everything comes back.

I tell you,
Someone will remember us
In the future.

So then picture
Us here, forever.
Not stamped ephemeral,
You know,
As hooves cast in snow.

Transcendence

Transcendence is buried in the earth,
But we look up.
Transcendence is dark yeasty gathering,
But we seek scattered clouds.
Transcendence is clay-like alchemy,
But we rise away from it.
Transcendence beats in the core,
                    Bloody and whole,
But we stand still and wait for it.

You are the Earth

You are the earth buried so deep inside me
It becomes a heartbeat.
I am muddy from my day and it feels good
To gallop home.
Rest is small birds darkened by trees.
Longing is night.
How day combs the strands of a young girl,
Night brings me home.
I am muddy and whole. I taste the earth at twilight,
And it envelops me too.

Which to Prefer

I do not know which to prefer,
The beauty of inflections
Or the beauty of innuendoes...
        —Wallace Stevens

The best is not
        after or inflection.
It is the hum
        of winter
Almost still
        in its vibration.
An iron-dark kettle perched
        on a fiery branch.
Flung full of sun.
        From black feathers,
Red radiation,
        mid-air meditation,
Before the steam
        has sung.

Prometheus's Monster

There's this cat
Called Prometheus
Who wants to
Skunk up my tree.

Gave me fire,
Creativity,
Then backed away—
Afraid of it, of me.

Prometheus, return to me.
I am your useful monster.
Set aflame
So prettily.

Pollination

It is all pollination—
Creation—
The most fertile place.
Deep recess,
Soft-petaled vibration,
Sun-steeped
Exploration, discovery.
Pollen on stamen.
We dust our feet with it,
Dance
The shape of language.
Hive and lace
Every surface, perfect,
Not surfeit.
Every barrier, an opening.
Geometric.
Slow rush of destiny within
Honeycomb.
Inflection of tongue, golden,
Brought to womb,
A room, inner chamber, a lair.
Percolation.
Every sweetness, every fruit,
Every root,
Owes itself to this obsession.
Each generation
Much improved by the last one.

What will happen
When we bees all die, are gone?
Optimism for bees'
Symbolism. Immortality—

New Roots

for Mary Oliver, in memory

Soft leaves, so small,
Cluster on newly naked
Stems. Let water bathe and
Caress each vulnerability.
Let sun breathe on them.

Growth will come. Don't let
This slowness burden you.
You've decided it's time.
That is enough for now.
Don't watch for every sign.

We draw our own connections.
A bounty of light rushes in,
Darkness too. Allows it to happen.
No visible tap root, revelations
Come where we're most open.

Roots will form again
In their own time. Trust
Nature's agenda, now that
You've helped it surely along—
You can only force so much.

Your Words

I want you
To speak to me,
In fact,
As you would speak
To your animals.

Because I want
To capture
That pure,
True animal
Of your words,
Pungent and alive.

Those
You don't need
To speak
Because they
Give softly,
Breathing
In the night.

Their
Visible scent
A glistening
Fever,
A ripe
Lurking,
As I lull them
Gently to sleep.

I Like When You Speak

I like when you speak. When you tell stories
That my distant self can recognize. That pull me in,
A living seduction of laughter and longing. As you breathe
And your cheeks turn pink, I want to kiss, but I listen.

You fill my soul with what is real.
More persistent than dreams. What I recognize
In a locked glance, the smooth feel
Of your neck, what you confide.

You speak your own words, and I don't take your silence,
Turn it into my own speech. I wait,
As is only right. No insistence
Because love can pause, hesitate, shyly brush my lips.

I like when you speak. When you are here
Saying all that you want to say, and nothing more.
When you are enveloping and near,
Or drawing me in from afar, a house with an open door.

Badass Mermaid

It is no night to drown in
        —*Lorelei* by Sylvia Plath

Blood whirls within
Whorl of ear—
Ocean's sound.
You, profound
And under deep.
Hobgoblin,
Hobbling.
Hobbling there
        Before I sleep.
I, in your realm.
A siren—
Not yet, but
Sobbing.

You,
Moving.
Murk,
Darkness,
Spy's lurk.

In winter,
I tumbled there,
Accidentally.

I sang
Within the sea.
Fathomed
I had privacy.

Your ears,
They bled
With my
Song.
Homer's
Odysseus
Told it wrong,
Or his men
Told it,
Innocent.
Their ears
Wax-sealed
Against
All sound.

I, innocent too,
Innocently
Fell asleep.
        Dry-iced
Packed
        In snow
That does not freeze.
        Leagues and leagues deep.
        Countless.

(Before that,
      Or after—
I don't remember,
      And probably pointless—
I used your shampoo.
      Smiled, and combed my hair.
Your rage silvered and glinted
      On your teeth and eye.
No matter, soon,
      Back home,
      Spring.
          Somehow, I didn't care.)

I slept
      Until I woke.

Chrysalis
      Cracked
On sea floor.
      I, a mermaid—with wings.
Lorelei. Butterfly.
      A terrible glistening.
      Beauty can be frightening.

I did not know myself.
      Knowing all
      I could know.
      My mind

A mantle
Ripped off
Like a sheet
At night
Became great,
                One
                Vast
                Eye.

Then I could write
        Like a seer:
        Everything and everywhere.
A messenger.

I do not drown.
        Badass Mermaid,
        I breathe
        Water,
                I breathe air.

I derange.

        Pitched roofs, pitched reefs.
I say your name, write your nightmare.
        Dive back under,
        Scaled with your fear.

My tail smacks down.
        Flashed lightning,
        Ear-rending thunder.

Irritated clam creates
The pearl.
The pearl, in turn, creates me.

Then I create.
Write.
Surrender.
Open a universe, land and sea.

What We Find

Sea this morning, a flattened pewter.
Hard and uncompromising.
Waves frozen, unmoving.
Beach combed of all shells, pebbles.
A barren wasteland of sand,
Driftwood scorched and scarred
By now dead fires.

Off in the distance, a whale exhales
Long-held breath, breaches,
Dives back under.
The only thing that can break
These strong waters
Into wakes of surrender.
The only thing that can sing
Its unique song.
The unique song that each of us sings.
Not on the surface,
Not in the light,
But there, in the deep,
There, in the darkness.

To find our direction,
Our own voice,
Each other.
To sing uniquely, but not alone.
Eerie electricity. Connection.
Through the song:
Everything is the right choice.

A Single Note in the Infinite

Flapped and whiplashed onto shore,
Then tenderly pulled back and within,
Like a child tucked into place at night.
But here, there are no stars,
And the sea slaps and washes
You clean of dreams.
Salt-beaten and cracked-lipped,
You pray against its blind thrash.
Smoothed like a pebble,
Opened like a shell.
Awake, awake.
Hungry prayer,
Angry fire of dying sun upon waves.
Honed and honed
To a perfect grain of sand.
Minute. A single note
In the infinite.

Water

Waiting out high tide—
Water, memory drifting
Over rocks, engulfing.
Then I decide to go for it,
Breathe in it, my body
Its own arched wave,
My mind its own sea.
Swirling darkness
Catches light. Water,
Unlanguaged mnemonic,
Also its own evocation.
Crashing flood that I ride.
Hallelujah.

New Moon
For Cecily

You died in the limbo
Of a new moon.
A blank sky, a blank slate.
Only 25.
There are those who believe
Had you lived,
You never would have tried
Again, but you
Stabbed yourself out of this life,
Like stars sear holes
Into our sky,
Like you gone sears holes
Into our lives
So that we move through
With reckless caution,
Upheaval and grief that we organize.
That we place
Item by item, memory by memory.
That we smooth
Into the earth with your straight,
Long limbs,
Perfect and young.
I think of you.
How you touched the blood
With your finger,
A last question in a night
So dark.

Standing in the Kitchen

Sometimes I suck the ghost of you
      From a plum at the sink.
Savor its skin against my lips,
      Tongue its soft flesh and juices.
Cry at the hard core, thick mass
      That within you grew,
Took you from me, all your beautiful ripeness.
      The sink drips its beat.
The incongruity of things that last:
      Silence, sound, impermanence.

What Comes After

All that's left:
Your name no longer
Your name, but another.

The greatness
Of each
Small power.

Nothing more than it is.
Perhaps simply nothing.
Given and not given.

Don't be afraid
Of your own
Leaving.

Don't be afraid
That you won't
Remember.

Someday
Your true name
Will answer.

Notes:

1. "Every Possible Thing" is responsive to the Anonymous poem, "Donal Og," translated by Lady Augusta Gregory.
2. "Emily and Susie" is inspired by the close romantic relationship between Emily Dickinson and her sister-in-law, Susan Huntington Gilbert Dickinson.
3. "Virginia" is about Virginia Woolf, and it is also a very personal piece, about my return to writing after a long creative silence.
4. "Not Stamped Ephemeral" borrows lines from "Sapphic Fragments," Julia Dubnoff's translation of a fragment of Sappho's verse:"I tell you,/Someone will remember us/In the future."
5. "Which to Prefer" is inspired by the lines quoted above it, from "Thirteen Ways of Looking at a Blackbird," by Wallace Stevens.
6. "Prometheus's Monster" takes from the myth of Prometheus, and also is in honor of Mary Shelley, author of the great novel *Frankenstein; or the Modern Prometheus.*
7. "Pollination" is on one level about bees, whom we rely on for much of our food supply. On another level, this poem is about human artists and creators.
8. "New Roots," dedicated to Mary Oliver, I wrote shortly after she passed away.
9. "I Like When You Speak" is responsive to Pablo Neruda's poem "Me gustas cuando callas/I like you when you're quiet." "Your Words" is in a similar vein.
10. "Badass Mermaid" is inspired by the German legend of the siren Lorelei, which has been portrayed in art song and other

music, as well as the poem "Lorelei," by Sylvia Plath. "Badass Mermaid" is also inspired by Madeline Miller's *Circe*. I see Lorelei as a powerful creatrix like Circe, whom some found dangerous.

11. "New Moon" is dedicated to my dear friend, the late Cecily Bostock, a polymath genius. In addition to her many other gifts, she was a brilliant poet.

12. "Every Possible Thing," "Emily and Susie," "Virginia," and "Prometheus's Monster" are being set to music for soprano in an art song cycle by composer extraordinaire Myron Silberstein. He is also composing separate works for "Pollination" and "New Roots."

CPSIA information can be obtained
at www.ICGtesting.com
Printed in the USA
LVHW051106280920
667265LV00007B/567